'Harry and the Egg' and other short stories

written by Susan Duxbury

Published by 'Books on Demand'

Copyright 2013
Susan Duxbury

Table of contents

Harry and the Egg.

Mr. Tiddles' Prize:

Two of a different kind

Uncle Lewis' Revenge.

The Short-Legged Flamingo

Harry and the Egg.

When people ask me how I find the energy to walk up that steep road, six-days-a-week and at my age, I offer them one of those Gobstoppers I keep in my pocket, those that change colour when you suck them. Mind you, I don't get them mixed up with the 'Wuffies' I also keep at the ready; a reliable distraction for vicious dogs, and those that insist upon licking your ears.

I start at the 'Moor Valley Spinners & Dyers Ltd', where registered mail must be signed by Miss Jackson, a charming lady who has been Mr. Chapman's secretary since I started walking up this Yorkshire hillside. I often stop at her office for a chat. When I mentioned that Nelly was taking classes on home-dressmaking, she gave me a beautiful length of finely woven mohair-tweed.

"It'll make a lovely skirt for your wife," she said.

I cross the bridge over the river, which looks even more picturesque now that the trees along the embankment are budding into different shades of green. Opposite the mill and built parallel to the river, are three streets of 'back to backs' where most of the workers live. To be honest, it took me a while to get used to the tongue-twisting names of those who have come from foreign countries to work here. Take Mr. and Mrs. Mikolaiwicz for example, living in old Grandma Mason's house along Alma Row. He works in the weaving and she is in the canteen. Now how can anyone get their tongue around a name like that?

Further up the road is the Catholic Church and good old Father McCarthy. At this time of the morning, he is usually out on some godly mission: driving his old Bentley and causing traffic-jams. I hand over the mail to Mary, his Irish housekeeper, who invariable enquires after my health, since I mentioned the doctors had advised me to get an outdoor job, because of gas that got into my lungs during the war.

Although I enjoy working as a postman, I must admit that the stage is my passion. You see, in my spare time, I'm a 'stand-up' comedian with the 'Happy Hours Concert-Party', which I've been with since it was founded, twenty years ago. Some say I'm a born clown, and even though I enjoy a bit of slapstick now and again, I strongly appreciate a good practical joke. For such purposes, I often borrow an odd item from the concert-party's prop-box; like the big-black-hairy-rubber-spider we used for the 'Miss Muffet sat on her tuffet' sketch. No, I never expected them to call the fire-brigade when they found it lodged between the mill's post.

At our open-air concert in the park last summer, I did a successful imitation of Charlie Chaplin, which gained much applause and a couple of encores. Of course, I couldn't resist wearing the baggy trousers the following day, and letting them drop as I handed Mrs. Saunders a letter from her daughter. Her eyeballs nearly fell out, when she saw my 'Union Jack' underpants. That had been a successful gag at the 'Soldiers and Sailors Annual Christmas Dinner' too.

Dave, who has been my good friend for many years, keeps a flock of about ten 'Rode Island Reds' at the top of a wooded hill behind his house, half-way up the road. On a Saturday morning, I always stop for a cup of tea; to talk about poultry-keeping and politics. Sometimes, on a Friday evening, we'll meet for a game of dominoes at the 'Junction'. I'll never forget when he told me his hens had gone off-laying. "If things don't improve, they'll end up in the pot!" he said, which made me suspect that he'd been at his elderberry-wine again. He *never* kills any of his hens, and I'm pretty sure he wouldn't eat them if he did. Then my thoughts turned to the concert party's prop-box, and I remembered the 'Ugly Duckling' sketch we did at the Sunday School picnic, last July.

...

Dave's wife had gone shopping when I arrived at their house that Friday morning.

At least *that*'s one hurdle got over, I thought, as I pushed the electricity bill through the letter box: and another when I discovered that the neighbours weren't home either. So nobody saw me climb those over-dimensional self-made steps leading up to the chicken-run, which are more suited to Dave's long legs than mine. It's a lovely spot up there. I do appreciate the pretty countryside around the village, the carpet of bluebells stretching down the hillside. Far below, between the branches of high trees, I could see a bright red double-decker bus, slowly rumbling up the road. Behind the hut is a disused quarry surrounded by a stone wall, where Dave hides the key.

Hens scattered in all directions. The cock flapped his wings menacingly as I carefully placed the contents of a large toffee tin between a couple of freshly laid eggs. They resembled those of a sparrow rather than a hen, in comparison to the one I'd borrowed from the concert-party's prop box. "That'll save you from the pot!" I informed the suspicious bird that pecked aggressively at the grotesque intrusion, and stared indignantly as I left the hut.

...

The unusual amount of activity in the vicinity of Dave's house didn't escape my notice, as I slowly worked my way up the hill the following morning. Then I saw the van, belonging to the local newspaper, parked opposite the house. It caused an uncomfortable twinge at the pit of my stomach.

"Come in Harry!" said Dave's wife, as I reached the door. "We have something to show you!" she added excitedly, and steered me into the parlour. It was full of people: mostly neighbours and a photographer who stood in the corner, grinning behind his camera fixed onto a tripod. Dave stood to attention; arms stiffly at his side and chin pushed forward, looking like one of those guards outside Buckingham Palace, who he claims are a 'sloppy lot' compared to a Royal Marine. He looked at me and smiled proudly, as he pointed to the huge white egg on a green velvet cushion in the centre of the table.

"It'll be in t 'Guinness Book of Records' will that," said George Bottomley, from number sixty-two.

"Ay! I've never seen owt like it in all me born days! It must 'ave taken some pushin' out, " said old Mr. Bradshaw, a well-known local authority on poultry-keeping. Which bird is responsible for that, then? Was it Bertha who'd been walking a bit funny?

Dave's wife pushed me towards the table. Before I knew, I was standing next to him.

"Hey listen Dave! I must explain something!" I whispered frantically. But Dave wasn't listening, he was still 'changing the guards' and thinking he was back in the 'Marines'.

"Say cheeeese!" said the photographer. Before I could gather my wits, there was a flash. I took a deep breath and opened my mouth. "Shurrup talking and smile, Harry!" said Fred Hopkins among a gathering crowd around the door. There was another flash and I opened my mouth again. Then they started talking and laughing. I couldn't get a word in edgeways, so I said there was still a lot of mail to be delivered, shouldered my mailbag, and elbowed my way out of the house.

...

It puzzles me how people change their moods for no apparent reason. One day they mumble a mere greeting, and the next day they are cheerful and smiling. This kind of behaviour I consider unreasonable, especially on a Monday morning when, according to the laws of human nature, people should be miserable.

Mrs. Winterbottom, who wouldn't laugh if you tickled her feet, managed to squeeze her face into the semblance of a smile, as she signed the receipt for a 'Country Ladies Book Club' parcel. To make matters worse, the distinguished John Glover, a retired solicitor's clerk, almost bent double when he saw me coming.

"Famous at last!" said Mrs. Coulton at the newsagents, and broke into peals of laughter as I entered the shop.

"People aren't supposed to laugh on Monday mornings!" I remarked stiffly, and handed over a letter from the Shire Council. Her earrings dangled rhythmically as she ignored the letter, took a newspaper from the pile on the counter and presented it to me as though it was some kind of trophy. Glaring from the bottom half of the front page, was a picture of yours truly, gawping into the camera behind a big white egg on a cushion.

"Harry the postman and his egg," it was captioned. I felt my jaw drop.

'Well known as an amateur comedian and famous for his practical jokes, Harry's attempts to foil Mr. David Dean into believing his hens had laid an outsize egg, rebounded this time.

"I knew he would be up to something when I told him my hens were off laying",

said Mr. Dean, who has known Harry since he started as a postman, twenty-five years ago.........'

Mrs. Coulton dried her eyes with a handkerchief and I put sixpence on the counter.

"Wait until Nelly sees this!" I said.

Mr. Tiddles' Prize:

I know you're wondering why I've stopped parking the car inside the garage. Yes, I agree, it doesn't make sense does it? - leaving a brand new car parked on the driveway, despite the bad weather.

I'll let you into a secret; I'm scared stiff of driving the car into the garage.

Why am I scared stiff of driving the car into the garage?

I'm scared stiff of driving the car into the garage, because there isn't enough room for five-hundred-and-fifty tins of cat-food, as well as the car.

Yes, you heard correctly! Five hundred- and -fifty tins of cat-food – and I don't fancy stacking them again either. It took me a whole day to get the job done, and my back is giving me hell.

Go on! Ask me how I got hold of five hundred-and-fifty tins of cat-food. I can tell by the expression on your face that you're dying to know.

Now just listen to this! You won't believe it, but it's true: It was the post-office. Yes, you heard correctly - the post office - not doing their job - as usual. If they had worked more efficiently I wouldn't be in this predicament, would I?

No, I'm not going mad!

You know you how much work we put into the Metropolitan Council questionnaire last year, offering reduced housing-rates to old-age-pensioners if they would pay annually instead of monthly. If I'd have known how many old-age-pensioners we have in this town, I'd have gone off sick. Yes I would; I'd have gone off sick. Can you imagine how many hundreds of letters we sent out?

It caused havoc at the post-office; it was like Christmas repeated, which proves what I say about including a stamped-addressed envelope and people will reply to anything.

They had to do overtime at the post-office, sorting all those return-replies; which is probably why they didn't put them all through the franking machine.

'Waste not, want not', Grandma used to say, bless her soul, which has become a lifelong motto of mine too. As I sat in the office during lunch-break, I could almost hear her cackling voice, reminding me not to be wasteful while I sorted those un-franked letters. Believe me! I actually forfeited a whole week of lunch breaks, peeling off stamps and cutting them out. Some of them must have been stuck on with propeller-glue because my fingertips were as red and raw as a bunch of radishes when I'd finished. But it was worth it. Oh yes, it was worth it alright! At the end of the week I took home a biscuit tin filled to the brim with re-cycled postage stamps.

And then, one evening, while I was opening Mr. Tiddles' tin of 'Natty Catty', I suddenly saw this picture of a diamond necklace on the label, and couldn't take my eyes off it. I have a soft spot for diamonds – they're definitely a girl's best friend, aren't they? Well! They would be my best friend if I had some. I've often dreamed of wearing a genuine diamond necklace and looking like Elizabeth Taylor – at least, just for a few minutes. And could you believe it? The only thing between me and that diamond necklace was a missing word in a silly sentence.

No doubt you've heard that silly '***Natty Catty' Gourmet Cat-Food'*** jingle a thousand times already. Aha! Gets on *your* nerves too, does it? You're quite right! –it's too repetitive and horribly irritating. I suppose you're like me and switch the thing off as soon as you hear that silly doodle-tune accompanied by high-pitched meowing. So you can believe me when I tell you, after I had finished writing 'NATTY CATS ARE HAPPY CATS' on two-hundred and fifty postcards - until the tin of stamps was empty – the only thing that kept me from going insane was imagining myself wearing that diamond necklace.

Nevertheless, days of sweet suspense bridged that tormenting gap until at last, the long awaited letter arrived. Can you imagine how excited I was? My hands actually trembled as I attempted to open two – *and I repeat not one, but two* - letters decorated with colourful tins of 'Natty Catty' next to grinning cats licking their lips.

As soon as I'd ripped open the first letter, I half expected a diamond necklace to fall out, which is quite ridiculous when you come to think about it, because who in their right mind would send a diamond necklace through the post? I read the letter, informing me I had won the second prize and a year's supply of 'Natty Catty'.

Never mind, I thought; here's the other letter informing me that I've won the first prize. It couldn't be anything else … or could it..?

As I opened the second letter, I saw Mr. Tiddles out of the corner of my eye, stretching himself comfortably on the velvet cushion in front of the fire. I could swear he was grinning when I told him we had not only won the second prize, but the third prize as well - and another six-month supply of 'Natty Catty'.

By the way, I'm wondering if there might there be some Cheshire-Cat in his lineage.

As the diamond necklace floated out of my imagination, good old Mr. Tiddles continued purring contentedly while I wondered where on earth I could stock five-hundred and forty-eight tins of cat-food.

At least it comes in six different flavours. Mr. Tiddles' favourite is 'Paw Lickin' Jellied Rabbit', but he does enjoy a dish of 'Fancy Feast Chicken and Herring' now and again.

The good news must have spread around the local cat-community like wild-fire, because it wasn't long before Mr. Tiddles appeared in the company of a friendly tortoise-shelled companion, with whom he generously shared his dish of 'Natural Balance Turkey and Salmon' and afterwards made her into 'Mrs. Tiddles'.

Now Mrs Tiddles prefers a hearty meal of 'Classic Beef-Cubes in Gravy' to anything else, but won't turn up her nose at a tin of 'Cats Nutritious Lamb Delicacy'. "Good food increases production", said Dr. Barking when I went to the local vet because of Mrs Tiddles' fat tummy. That was three months ago. Now, six beautifully marked kittens are feeding their way through the garage stock. They prefer 'Pork Chunks in Brown Sauce' to the 'Vitamin-Enriched 'Creamy-Fish-Balls for Kittens', which just goes to prove that television commercials don't tell the truth.

Would you care to meet Family Tiddles?

Open the garage and they'll appear like a shot! Don't ask me how they do it, but it never fails. Do you think it might be telepathy, or just the squeaky door they can hear?

Like I said, look who's coming around the corner! Mr. Tiddles is taking the lead as usual, proud and handsome in his freshly-licked black and white fur-coat. And here she is, Mrs Tiddles, badly in need of fortification after looking after her large family. Just watch that little black and white bundle of energy having a go at the drainpipe again; and that tiny tortoiseshell with its nose into the bucket. Naughty pussy, you'll get your paws wet!

Do me a favour and keep your eye on that grey and white one over there, trying to run up the laburnum while I retrieve the garden-rake from that tortoise-shelled mischief-maker.

Oops! Too late! There it goes!

Let's see what's on today's menu, shall we?

Two of a Different Kind.

It wasn't easy finding a new place to live. At least they could have waited until summer, before throwing me out of the car window and onto the pavement in a cloud of exhaust fumes and leaving me to fend for myself.

I sat on people's window-sills and yowled to be let in, but they chased my away. Then I worked out how to catch young rabbits before they noticed me coming up behind. Sometimes I managed to open the odd dustbin lid, but in the end, preferred catching my own food, especially the mice which are fun to play with before being eaten. You can toss them into the air and catch them; let them run off before pouncing on them for another game of dash and grab.

It's easy to find a warm, sheltered place if you know where to look. But it did take a while before I found my new people.

I lapped up warm milk in a place that was soft and warm and friendly which made me purr - and that was something I hadn't done for a while. The new people made friendly noises and stroked my back although I sensed there must be some hook about it. And sure enough, there it was; the animal they called Charlie entered the room. I had already picked up his scent a couple of times already, but never been so close to the likes of him before. He had the audacity to poke his nose into my fur and bark, so I lashed out with open claws and made fierce hissing noises to show I could defend myself if I had to. After that, we were never good friends, Charlie and I.

My new people made a hole in the door through which I could come inside and sleep next to the oven when I had finished checking-out my territory. And a terrific territory it was too! All I had to do was choose a scented hole and sit quietly, waiting for my next meal to appear.

I love any kind of game, but Charlie would never play games with me; not even if I jumped over him when he was asleep on the rug, or take a swipe at his tail – a game I remember playing with my sisters before they disappeared.

Now don't get me wrong! I don't mind taking second place inside the house as long as nobody interferes with my territory outside, where I am the indisputable boss. If a randy male dares to enter my area and bother my ladies, I'll howl him into merciless capitulation; especially at springtime when I feel the need to satisfy my desires.

But I never did that to Charlie, who was a real son-of-a-bitch about food. Occasionally, I would show my respect by leaving him a few morsels of meat in my dish, which went down his throat as fast as a rabbit in a hole. You'd think he might have returned the favour, wouldn't you? But not mean old Charlie! He would gulp down his food and then start on mine; and once he'd got started he wouldn't leave off.

Not only was Charlie as mean as hell about his food, it was the same with the couch. He growled me off before I could even get up, so I ignored him and jumped up at the far end. Then I started playing my tricks, which I can't resist now and again, crawling towards him as slowly as I could, getting closer and closer, until he got mad and snapped. Considering he was only half my size and with teeth like a mouse, I could have wiped him off like a bug on a rug had I wanted; but I wouldn't have done a nasty thing like that because I like my people and my people liked Charlie, so I watched my step because he was there first.

After many seasons, Charlie began to smell old and our people carried him around instead of letting him walk. I always show consideration to those about to depart, and reckon I did him a last favour by placing a field-mouse in front of his paws for the kill. He really did enjoy shaking it dead. Charlie ran across the lawn looking mighty proud of himself, because our people were clapping their hands and making loud noises. Then he allowed me to sit next to him on the sun-bed, but only for a short while, mind you!

When I came through the hole the following morning, I knew straight away that something had died. Sure enough, there was a towel over Charlie's basket and a lifeless pile of brown hair underneath.

After Charlie had been put into a deep hole at the bottom of the garden, life became more relaxed. No longer did I need to hurry, lapping up the milk and emptying my dish, with old Charlie standing next to me and waiting to butt in. I could take my time about everything; I could even fall asleep on the couch if I pleased.

Now I'm the undisputed boss around the area. A big, strong, tom-cat like me doesn't take any nonsense. But all the same, I do miss annoying old Charlie although he was well and truly the son-of-a-bitch.

Uncle Lewis' Revenge·

It took me a long time to figure out how Uncle Lewis had got inside that black box, which Mum kept in the kitchen cupboard on the top shelf.

At first I was sure those men in black suits had squeezed him inside, after taking him out of the big box in which they had carried him into the house.

It was all a big joke, of course. Uncle Lewis had promised to take us for a ride in his brand-new red sports car and I was sure he was playing one of his tricks , so I waited for him to jump-out. Uncle Lewis loved scaring people, especially me and my two older sisters.

But when they heaved the big box onto the table, Uncle Lewis stayed inside. People were moaning and weeping which was very disturbing. I remember thinking it was because the box was too heavy. People I knew came into the room. They went out again, shaking their heads and looking like black shadowy ghosts with faces like chalk, which scared us no end. Others sat around the box in silence and Mum told us to go upstairs and stay there.

We sat on the landing with our heads through the banisters. There was the photo of Uncle Lewis in a silver frame on the sideboard below. He was wearing a black gown, a funny flat hat, with a roll of paper in his hand like it was something very precious. I could swear he was looking up the stairs and grinning at us.

"The car's a complete write-off," I heard somebody say.

...

I really and truly hated it when people got mad with Mum. Some said she was morbid and others called her stubborn. I hated it even more when Dad packed his suitcase and left.

Mum said he'd gone to live with his new family.

At least Uncle John, our favourite uncle, visited us regularly. He and Mum always sat at the kitchen table having serious conversations which we didn't understand. I'll never forget the afternoon when Uncle John banged his fist on the table and made a loud noise. The blue and white fruit-bowl we had bought with our pocket money for Mum's birthday fell from the table and onto the tiles. While I was trying to piece it together, I overheard Mum say she couldn't bear the thought of Lewis being put into the cold and damp earth. That was when Uncle John stood up and left the house without saying good-bye. We never saw him again.

At lease Aunt Priscilla still came quite often. She wore elegant clothes and smelt very nice, so I didn't mind her sleeping in my room. I moved in with Mandy who warmed my feet and scratched my back while we tried to make out what they were talking about, in the room directly below.

Mandy and I were horrified when Aunt Priscilla started shouting and Mum started screaming. "You were always jealous of Lewis," we heard Aunt Priscilla say as she came up the stairs and a short time later, went down again. So we got out of bed and sat on the landing, watching Aunt Priscilla through the banisters, putting on her fur coat and leaving the house, slamming the door behind her.

We never saw Aunt Priscilla again either.

After that, we didn't have any more visitors…

I started high-school when Mandy began wearing a bra and Jane plastered her face with make-up. She fancied Larry Parker and kept going into swoons, which didn't seem to bother Mum in the slightest.

"I've got a full-time job," she announced one day, and added that she expected us to do the housework because she had no time. We could eat school dinners and do our homework after finishing the chores, she said, which bore no discussion. There was no questioning of facts, adolescent protests or teenage revolts. It was useless quarrelling with Mum when she had made up her mind.

We succumbed to our fate. Half-hearted attempts at mowing the lawn, washing, ironing, cleaning and shopping, developed, as we grew older, into a well organised logistical system. It enabled us to do our chores and produce satisfactory school results, while Mum ran the local library.

On a cold and rainy afternoon, we started playing with Uncle Lewis.

Jane took him down from the top shelf and placed him on the kitchen table next to a lighted candle; switched off the lamp and walked around the table. Her eyes were fixed on the black box which seemed to radiate a dark glow in the reflecting flame, flickering dark shadows on the wall and dancing in currents of air. Then she gave Uncle Lewis a detailed description of what she and Larry Parker had done behind the rowing-club hut. I was suddenly scared he might get disgusted and come out of his box, so I hid behind the curtains and watched the rain making puddles on the lawn.

"Oh! I don't believe it! Did you really show him your boobs?" squealed Mandy who could get hysterical at times. She danced after Jane who looked smug and secretive. Then I ran out of the room in shame and took refuge in my wardrobe.

"It's your turn to play with Uncle Lewis," said Jane to Mandy. It was Autumn Break and we had finished the housework. Mum was still at the library. Mandy took Uncle Lewis out of the cupboard to read him some hot passages from ''Lady Chatterly's

Lover', which Mum had borrowed from the library and we'd found under her bed.

Then it was my turn, so I quoted an article from the 'Playboy' entitled 'How to have sex on a crowded beach without being noticed", in the hope that this might just be the thing for Uncle Lewis.

All in all, we had a great time with Uncle Lewis and sincerely hope he enjoyed himself too.

One Sunday afternoon after a particularly horny session, Jane said, "Who dares to take Uncle Lewis to school?"

I am ashamed to admit we got hysterical again, and argued noisily about who had the guts to carry out the challenge; then we pulled sticks, and I won.

The following morning, I packed Uncle Lewis into the bottom of my bag, ready for his first day at school and being permanently broke, I charged for a look. With the exception of Molly Brian who was my best friend, everybody forfeited something for a peep at Uncle Lewis. Then Miss Montgomery, our Maths teacher and as humourless as a dried up pond, entered the classroom during the eleven o' clock break and saw the crowd around my desk. Her eyes bulged like a bull-frog when she saw Uncle Lewis in the box and sent me home with an official letter addressed to Mum.

After that, Uncle Lewis disappeared from the kitchen cupboard and it was a long time before we saw him again.

...

Mandy had flown over from Canada where she worked as a biologist at a research centre in Winnipeg. Jane had driven up from the south, where she lived with her husband and three children. I had recently obtained a degree in local government and had found a job at the Treasury Department of a neighbouring council. We had come to clear the house that was no longer our home; where Mum had lived alone for the past ten years, until a sudden heart-attack had taken her into hospital, from which she never returned.

"Say hello to Uncle Lewis!" said Jane, triumphantly, holding up the neatly wrapped parcel. "I've just found him in a hat box, under that ghastly red hat Mum wore at someone's wedding and kept as a trophy".

Jane's eyes gleamed with contagious mischief and suddenly, we put aside our sorrow. We were young girls again, dancing in circles around a room filled with relics of the past; once treasured and precious, now just one stage before the rubbish tip, and ready to be forgotten.

Mandy stood still and regarded us seriously. "We'll have to bury old Lewis," she said, as though announcing the inevitable.

"Of course we must!" I agreed.

"Poor Uncle Lewis! He should really be rewarded for all that crap he took," said Mandy, having developed a strong sentimental streak over the years.

"Let's take him out for a meal before we get rid of him," Jane suggested.

"Nothing but the best will do for old Lewis! We'll take him to the 'Mayfair'," I said.

Then we disappeared into our bedrooms to dress for the occasion.

...

I couldn't help thinking there was something strangely familiar about the handsome waiter who escorted us to a corner table in the Mayfair's unusually empty dining-room. A cynical smile displayed the gap between two strong front teeth and his hair, quaintly parted down the middle, fell into thick waves at each side of his forehead. He presented us with leather-bound and gold scrolled menu-cards;

whisked an imaginary crumb from the spotlessly white tablecloth and ignored the black box which Jane had discreetly placed on the empty chair at the head of the table.

We exchanged knowing glances and grinned. The waiter smiled politely, unperturbed by the chorus of giggles, rapidly developing into hysterical laughter.

"Might I suggest 'Coq au Escargot," he said patiently, his voice soft and distant.

We snivelled and blew our noses, in an unsuccessful attempt to read the menu.

"Bring Uncle Lewis a large T-bone steak with plenty of baked potatoes. He hasn't eaten for years!" said Jane in a quavering voice. Our shoulders shook with suppressed laughter. The waiter nodded understandingly and headed towards the kitchen while our emotions ran free. Tears of mirth rolled down our faces.

"He's cute!" Mandy stuttered, opened her serviette and dabbed at trickles of mascara.

"A bit old fashioned," said Jane, her voice still trembling.

The food, which didn't seem so important any more, appeared before us as though served by an invisible hand, while we struggled in vain to control our emotions. Lumps of rubbery meat swam in grey sauce; we spat them out and deposited them on the rims of our plates making them look like clock-figures. Mandy screeched and held up her fork. She had jabbed it into a shapeless object with two rubbery horns. "It's a snail!" she announced and wailed in disgust.

"We should have ordered something else," I said helplessly. The plate at the head of the table was already empty and almost as clean as a whistle and I wondered who had eaten Uncle Lewis' steak. But it was no use asking Jane, who seemed absorbed with the bright-yellow feather dangling from her ear, and Mandy never spoke while renewing her lipstick.

As the waiter silently cleared the table, I opened my mouth and searched for the words that should have come, but didn't. How could I lodge a dignified complaint with tears of mirth still rolling down my face?

None of us spoke a word when we left the restaurant and walked home.

…

We were ill that night. Stomachs ached and intestines heaved. We moved backwards and forwards down the garden path looking like grotesque shadows in night-gowns, hurrying through the freezing rain to reach to the brick-house toilet on time. When we came back inside we were wet through and shivering with cold; we were also unable to sleep.

"Mum always kept her liver-salts in the kitchen cupboard. Perhaps they're still there," said Mandy. She heaved herself stiffly onto a chair and slid open the wood-panelled doors of the old-fashioned cupboard; a solitary remnant in an empty kitchen of bygone days.

"Look what I've found," she announced triumphantly, holding a white tin in one hand and a large brown envelope in the other. "It was jammed behind the shelf."

She opened the envelope and took out a photograph. We gazed silently at the familiar face; a handsome young man dressed in the robes of a university graduate, proudly holding his degree, a roll of paper in his hand. A cynical smile displayed the gap between two strong front teeth and his hair, quaintly parted down the middle, fell into thick waves at each side of his forehead. At the bottom right hand corner was written in spidery letters, "To my dear sister- with love, Lewis."

Dispirited and fearful, we pondered over questions without finding the answers, huddled together in the empty kitchen, in an empty house, dark and silent and no longer our home,. Now relieved that dawn had turned into daylight, we dressed absentmindedly and left the house to retrace our steps of the previous evening.

A workman appeared through the open doors of the restaurant that was no longer a restaurant, pushing a wheelbarrow filled with debris. We stared numbly at the hive of activity; covered our ears to shut out the deafening noise of a jack-hammer eating its way through the building. Jane said it was no use standing around. She took the large brown envelope from her bag and walked towards the workman who set down his wheelbarrow to study the photograph.

"Never seen 'im before my love," said the workman, scratching his head.

"But he served us with a meal yesterday evening!" There were traces of panic in Jane's voice.

"You must be a bit mixed up love," said the puzzled workman, "this has been a building-site since it burnt down a month ago."

"But we were here yesterday," I added faintly.

"We can't have dreamt it," said Mandy from the folds of her handkerchief because she had burst into tears.

Men stopped work and silently watched us running from one empty wall to the other, frantically searching for silk wallpaper bordered with gold; striding over piles of rubble where brightly coloured oriental carpets had been. Where were those sparkling crystal lamps? How could they possibly have disintegrated into dismal strips of cable hanging from the wall? And what about those beautiful brocade curtains behind matching pelmets?

A workman mumbled something about crazy women and the others laughed. There was the starting-up sound of a distant cement mixer; the jack-hammer continued its journey through stone floors.

…

Arm in arm, we walked slowly down the gravel path between weather-beaten graves. In front of us, the young parish vicar bearing the small black box on a richly embroidered cushion. A solemn church-warden stood by the tiny grave and a sudden breeze swirled around the graveyard, as Uncle Louis was given to the earth.

And what about Mum?

I can't bear the thought of poor old Mum in the cold damp earth. There's a fitted cupboard with sliding doors in the kitchen of my house, and a small black box on the top shelf.

I think I'll keep her there for a while.

The Short-Legged Flamingo

A feeling of deep satisfaction overcame Matthew as he gazed at the thick-lettered headline and read the caption under the photograph, covering half a side of the local newspaper.

At least she'll be well looked-after he thought, as he carefully folded the page and put it in his jacket pocket, imagining the hullabaloo it would cause. He could hardly wait to tell the tale to his mates at the 'Malt and Shovel'.

He left the house, crossed the stone-slab yard and opened the back gate next to the outhouse leading into Albert Road.

A bit early for the pub, he decided after consulting the silver pocket-watch, presented to him in appreciation of thirty-five years of sorting wool, although it hadn't helped him find another job after they had closed down the mill.

Emily had been upset of course. It had been the first year they hadn't been able to afford a holiday in Blackpool and so they had bought the allotment instead. It was there he was heading for now; to make sure there were no snails in his early lettuces.

He walked down the road towards the river, past the streets of soot-grimed terrace houses leading off Albert Road. Each of them bore the names of the Victorian entrepreneur's many children, who had built the mill, and then the model village to house its workers. West Yorkshire historians of the patriotic kind, claim it to be the cradle of the industrial revolution.

Rows of chimneys belched smoke into the darkening sky as villagers settled down for the evening. The penetrating odour of fried fish and vinegar drifted past his nostrils as he looked into 'Conny's Fish-and-Chip

Shop' and grunted a greeting to the group of customers waiting to pick up their evening meal, their complexions jaundiced by electric light-bulbs against bright yellow walls.

"Ello Matt! Ow-yer-goin' lad?" A man wearing a flat-cap and overalls stood in a doorway, smoking a pipe

"Fine thanks George! See yer later!" Matthew replied cheerfully.

He walked down the middle of the road and his boots clattered on the cobbles, there being no traffic at that time of the evening, except a couple of cars parked outside the off-licence on the corner of James Street. Next to the school, wrought-iron shutters barred 'Watson's Tobacconist and Sweet-Shop', whose affluence was growing rapidly with hoards of pupils in-navy-blue school uniforms. They invaded the village during the day and ate penny tea-cakes every morning at half-past-ten, delivered on big wooden trays from the village baker. After the bell, the village became a closed community once more, watched over by two great stone lions resting on high pillars at each side of the school entrance.

Before reaching the river, Matthew turned along a path that took him past the sculptured stone-walls of the Congregational Church, and into a large field chequered with neat rows of vegetables and dug-over plots. Dots of tiny huts defiantly faced the abandoned giant of a mill; the empty monumental building on the banks of the river which had once enveloped three generations of villagers for twelve hours a day and six days a week, and spat them into the church on the seventh. It stood there now, degraded into a sad remnant of lost wealth and patiently awaiting the decision of board-room magnates.

When Matthew took the key from his pocket, his finger touched the newspaper which reminded him of the story and he laughed inwardly. He opened the rickety door he had knocked together last summer, out of pieces of timber found in a mill-corner,

In the empty stall, there was nothing to remind him of previous occupants, except the straw-covered floor and a trough in the corner. He and Edith had sat in the kitchen until the early hours of Christmas Eve and his wife had said she could think of better things to do than sit there with red hands and raw finger-tips, pulling quills out of goose-flesh and knee deep in feathers. He examined his own hands, permanently ingrained from hundreds of bales of greasy raw wool, and remembered how scratched they had been too.

But he was glad he had saved Freda, although she'd been worse than a 'Pit Bull' while protecting her flock. He had felt a secret admiration for this brave mothergoose and would gladly have eaten a Christmas dinner of dry bread and cheese to save her from the ultimate fate of a well-fed bird.

Emily had been upset at first; had called him a silly old fool when he'd talked about buying an alien turkey from the market instead; but had quietened down after they had delivered Freda's flock and booked a three-day-trip to Blackpool on the proceeds.

He didn't regret for a minute, having released Freda from her loneliness. It was no life for a solitary goose at the bottom of a garden and would have been an act of grace, putting her out of her misery. His conscience began to rob him of his sleep and there had been no solution to his problem with Freda, until the afternoon he had sat in the kitchen, idly watching his grandson painting pictures. He'd seen the flamingo in the drawing-book; watched the boy dipping his paintbrush into a pot of bright pink water and the idea had hit him like a streak of lightning.

...

Early the next morning, he boarded the bus into town, paid the conductor and ignored curious stares at the huge wicker basket he was carrying. Freda let off a loud cackle now and again, although largely preoccupied with her pale pink feathers more than anything else. Thank goodness they had dried before she'd noticed his activities with the paint-brush.

No! He didn't regret what he had done, taking her to the park and throwing her over the wire-netting fence to join the other flamingos. He would tell the lads and they would have a good laugh, no doubt.

He made his way to the 'Malt and Shovel'. The folded newspaper was still in his pocket

...

"Hey! Now just listen to this! Now this is true is this!" Matthew held up a finger to make himself heard above the noise; to emphasise that he was telling the truth, the whole truth and nothing but the truth.

Somebody complained that he couldn't hear himself think and the noise died down because everybody knew that Matthew could tell a good tale.

He balanced precariously on a bar-room chair and having gained their attention, took the newspaper out of his pocket. Underlining his gestures with the necessary dramatic, he opened it slowly for all to see.

"Look at this!" Like a conjurer about to do a vanishing trick he showed the audience the newspaper clipping titled *'The short-legged flamingo'.* "That's our Freda painted pink!" said Matthew. He pointed at Freda, contentedly picking the ground between stilt-legged companions, which in turn, were gazing suspiciously at the new-comer.

There was a sudden roar and the raising of glasses. Somebody in the far-corner yelled at the 'daft so-and-so' to examine the date on the top right-hand corner.

Matthew examined the page. "The first of April," he read out loud.

"April fool, Matthew!"

...

Other books written by Susan Duxbury are –

'Up The Gum Tree'

'Buschleben'

'The Devil's Clown'

Published by Books on Demand.

Available September, 2015

'Little Germany: A History of Bradford's Germans' –

published by Amberley Publishing plc.

Herstellung und Verlag:
BoD - Books on Demand, Norderstedt
ISBN 978-3-7347-8151-3

MIX
Papier aus verantwortungsvollen Quellen
Paper from responsible sources
FSC® C105338